How to solve sudoku

How to solve sudoku

A step-by-step guide

Robin Wilson

Sterling Publishing Co., Inc.
New York

The right of Robin Wilson to be identified as the author of this book has been asserted in accordance with the Copyright, Designs and Patents Act 1988.

10 9 8 7 6 5 4 3

Published in 2006 by Sterling Publishing Co., Inc.
387 Park Avenue South, New York, NY 10016

First published in the UK in 2005 by The Infinite Ideas Company Limited
36 St. Giles, Oxford, England OX1 3LD
© 2005 by The Infinite Ideas Company Limited

Distributed in Canada by Sterling Publishing
C/o Canadian Manda Group, 165 Dufferin Street
Toronto, Ontario, Canada M6K 3H6

Sterling ISBN-13: 978-1-904902-62-1
       ISBN-10: 1-904902-62-6

For information about custom editions, special sales, premium and corporate purchases, please contact Sterling Special Sales Department at 800-805-5489 or specialsales@sterlingpub.com.

Designed and typeset by Baseline Arts Ltd, Oxford
Printed by TJ International, Cornwall

Contents

Preface

The sudoku craze has hit the western world with a vengeance.

Like other puzzles based on a square grid (such as crosswords and chess problems), a sudoku puzzle can be easy, or it can be a challenge to test the most committed of puzzlers. Like the Rubik cube a generation earlier, it has succeeded in catching the imagination of young and old alike, and is used in schools to teach logical thinking.

Much of the reason for its popularity stems from the fact that the basic rules are so very simple. Given a 9 x 9 grid divided into nine 3 x 3 mini-grids (boxes) and with some numbers already placed in it, fill in the rest of the grid in such a way that no number appears twice in the same row, column or box.

In spite of the appearance of numbers in these puzzles, no knowledge of maths is required. This is not an arithmetical puzzle, but rather a logic one, requiring only logical thinking, perseverance and patience.

This book differs from other sudoku books. Most of these start with a few pages of explanation and hints for solution, and then present a large collection of puzzles to be solved.

In contrast, this book concentrates on how to solve sudoku puzzles. It presents a systematic approach to their solution, starting with the easiest puzzles and gradually progressing to much harder ones, with useful tips, suggestions and nuggets of information along the way.

It should thus be ideal both for the beginner and also for the many thousands of people who have tried sudoku puzzles for fun but who have become stuck or would like to improve their solution skills.

Sudoku puzzles can be a lot of fun. We hope that this book will help you enjoy them even more.

Robin Wilson

Part 1

Introduction

1. What is sudoku?

Sudoku is a number puzzle usually consisting of a 9 x 9 grid (nine rows and nine columns), divided into nine 3 x 3 boxes, into which a few numbers have already been placed.

Here is an example:

				3		6		
4		5	8			1		
6		7	9					8
		4						
			1	2	3			
						7		
7					1	5		2
		6			7	8		9
		8		4				

The object of the puzzle is to fill in all the remaining squares with the numbers from 1 to 9, so that:

- *each row contains all the numbers from 1 to 9;*
- *each column contains all the numbers from 1 to 9;*
- *each 3 x 3 box contains all the numbers from 1 to 9.*

Notice that each of the numbers from 1 to 9 must appear just once in each row, once in each column, and once in each 3 x 3 box.

2. What makes a good puzzle?

A well-constructed sudoku puzzle has only one solution, and to find it you should be able to proceed in a logical step-by-step manner.

As you'll see, the puzzles can vary in difficulty from the easy to the extremely hard, depending on how many starting numbers are given, and where they're placed.

No calculations or arithmetical ability are needed. Indeed, some sudoku puzzles use letters (or other symbols) instead of numbers. It's entirely a test of logic, but one that may require much perseverance and patience.

Here's the solution to the puzzle on page 2 – later we'll go through the stages that lead to this solution (on pages 60–68).

9	8	1	5	3	2	6	7	4
4	2	5	8	7	6	1	9	3
6	3	7	9	1	4	2	5	8
3	1	4	7	6	8	9	2	5
5	7	9	1	2	3	4	8	6
8	6	2	4	9	5	7	3	1
7	9	3	6	8	1	5	4	2
2	4	6	3	5	7	8	1	9
1	5	8	2	4	9	3	6	7

Before you continue, you may like to check that each of the numbers from 1 to 9 appears just once in each row, once in each column, and once in each 3 x 3 box.

3. Why 'sudoku'?

Despite its name, sudoku isn't of Japanese origin. It seems to have originated in New York in the late 1970s, when Dell Magazines, an established American publisher of puzzles, included some sudoku-like puzzles in their magazine *Math Puzzles and Logic Problems* under the name of 'number place'.

The puzzles didn't reach Japan until the mid-1980s. The puzzle company Nikoli had seen an American number place problem and introduced it to the readers of their puzzle magazine, *Monthly Nikolist*, in April 1984. They gave the problem the snappy title *Sunji wa dokushin ni kagiru* (translated literally as 'number is limited only single'). This was soon shortened to *sudoku* (or *su doku*) – roughly speaking, 'su' means number and 'doku' means single.

It took some time for sudoku puzzles to become established in Japan. In 1986, Nikoli introduced two general rules for their puzzles:

■ the arrangement of numbers should be symmetrical – if you rotate the puzzle through 180°, the pattern of filled-in squares (though not the numbers) remains the same;

■ the number of filled-in squares should be limited to 30.

From that moment onwards, sudoku took off in Japan. It still remains highly popular, with five publishers currently producing monthly sudoku magazines for over half a million readers.

4. Sudoku hits the world

The sudoku craze first hit the UK in late 2004.

Wayne Gould, a retired High Court Judge living in Hong Kong, discovered sudoku in a Tokyo puzzle book in 1997. He then spent the next few years on and off designing computer programs to produce sudoku puzzles. He provides his puzzles to newspapers around the world.

In 2004 Gould sent a sudoku puzzle to *The Times* in London, which published its first puzzle on 12 November. These puzzles still appear, in four levels of difficulty (easy, mild, difficult and fiendish). Three days later, the *Daily Mail* introduced sudoku under the name 'Codenumber'.

By Easter 2005 a huge cottage industry had developed. On 16 May, the *Guardian*'s G2 section, 'home of the discerning sudoku addict', included a sudoku puzzle on every page, claiming that, 'as opposed to the risibly inferior versions spewed out by computer programs ... every puzzle in G2 today has been lovingly etched by a black-belt sudoku master on the upper slopes of Mount Fuji.'

By this time most other British papers had joined the bandwagon, competing with each other to offer prizes for solutions to sudoku puzzles of ever-increasing complexity and originality.

Since its first appearance, the puzzle has travelled the world, with addicts as widely spread as the United States, Europe, Asia and Australia.

It is true that some countries have so far failed to succumb – but it's just a matter of time...

Part 2

The basics

5. Getting started

In this part you'll encounter the basic techniques that you need to solve the most straightforward sudoku puzzles. There are initially three of these (others will follow later):

- scanning the rows
- scanning the columns
- filling in the gaps

Some other guides to sudoku introduce these techniques all at once. Here we prefer to take things more slowly and introduce them one at a time. However, once you've met and practised them you'll be able to use these methods interchangeably, choosing whichever one seems most helpful at the time.

In this part we'll work through a couple of sudoku puzzles in full, giving you a few questions to answer on the way. Following this you'll find some puzzles to try on your own. By the time you've worked through these, you should be able to solve straightforward sudoku puzzles.

A word of warning before we proceed. When trying to solve a sudoku puzzle, always remember that each step must be carried out logically. *Don't guess.* If you do, and you guess wrongly, you may find yourself having to go right back to the beginning.

Finally: *use a pencil, and keep an eraser handy.*

6. The basic language

The 9 x 9 array of numbers is the **grid**, containing 81 small squares, or **cells**. The grid is divided into nine **boxes**, numbered **1**, **2**, **3**, ... , **9** from top-left to bottom-right, each with nine cells.

The nine rows are lettered *A*, *B*, ... , *I*, and the nine columns are lettered *a*, *b*, ... , *i*. Cells are denoted by their row and column letters; for example, the cell in row *C* and column *g* (containing 4) is called *Cg*.

Before we go any further just check you understand the notation. *In the grid opposite:*

(i) *What is the number in cell Fb? In cell Ei?*

(ii) *Which cells contain the number 1?*

(iii) *Which rows and columns correspond to box* **8** *?*

(The answers are given below.)

	a	b	c	d	e	f	g	h	i
A	9					7		1	
B		7	4			2		6	5
C		1		8	9		4		
D	2				8		5	9	
E	1			2		3			6
F		4	5		1				2
G			7		4	1		2	
H	3	2		9			8	5	
I		6		5					7

Answers

(i) 4, 6 (ii) *Ah, Cb, Ea, Fe, Gf*

(iii) *Rows G, H, I and columns d, e, f*

7. Scanning the rows: 1

So, how might we go about solving the puzzle
on the previous page? Here is the grid again, for
easy reference.

	a	b	c	d	e	f	g	h	i
A	9					7		1	
B		7	4			2		6	5
C		1		8	9		4		
D	2				8		5	9	
E	1			2		3			6
F		4	5		1				2
G			7		4	1		2	
H	3	2		9			8	5	
I		6		5					7

First look at highlighted rows *D, E, F* (boxes **4**, **5**, **6**). In these three rows, each number from 1 to 9 must appear three times in total, once in each row and once in each box.

Notice that:

- ■ 2 already appears in three of these cells: *Da* (box **4**), *Ed* (box **5**) and *Fi* (box **6**);
- ■ 1 is in rows *E* (box **4**) and *F* (box **5**) so in box **6**, 1 must appear in row *D* – the only available cell is *Di (fill it in now)*;
- ■ 5 is in rows *F* (box **4**) and *D* (box **6**) so in box **5**, 5 must appear in row *E* – the only available cell is *Ee (fill it in now)*.

This process is called *scanning the rows for pairs.* We're looking for numbers that appear twice to see where the third appearance of that number must be. As you'll note, it can also be used in some cases where the number appears only once, but for that we need some extra information.

8. Scanning the rows: 2

Our grid is now as follows – the added numbers
are in a different font.

	a	b	c	d	e	f	g	h	i
A	9					7		1	
B		7	4			2		6	5
C		1		8	9		4		
D	2				8		5	9	*1*
E	1			2	*5*	3			6
F		*4*	5		1				2
G			7		4	1		2	
H	3	2		9			8	5	
I		6		5					7

We next look at rows *A*, *B*, *C* (boxes ■1■, ■2■, ■3■)
Fill in the numbers as you go.

■ 9 is in rows *A* (box ■1■) and *C* (box ■2■) so in
box ■3■, 9 must be in row *B* – the only
possibility is *Bg;*

■ 4 is in rows *B* (box ■1■) and *C* (box ■3■) so in
box ■2■, 4 must be in row *A*, in cell *Ad* or *Ae*;
but 4 is already in column *e* (in cell *Ge*), so
the only possibility is cell *Ad;*

■ 5 is in cell *Bi* (box ■3■); in box ■2■, 5 cannot be
in row *B* or in cell *Ad* (which now contains 4)
or *Ae* (because 5 is already in column *e*, in
cell *Ee*) – so 5 must be in column *f*, in cell *Cf;*
in box ■1■, 5 must then be in row *A*, in cell *Ab*
or *Ac* – but it can't be *Ac* (because 5 is
already in column *c*, in cell *Fc*), so the only
possibility is cell *Ab.*

9. Scanning the rows: 3

Our grid is now as follows:

	a	b	c	d	e	f	g	h	i
A	9	*5*		*4*		7		1	
B		7	4			2	*9*	6	5
C		1		8	9	*5*	4		
D	2				8		5	9	1
E	1			2	5	3			6
F		4	5		1				2
G			7		4	1		2	
H	3	2		9			8	5	
I		6		5					7

Questions

■ Look at rows *A, B, C. Where do the remaining 7s, 1s, 8s and 2s need to go?*

■ Look at rows *G, H, I* (boxes **7**, **8**, **9**). *In which cells should the remaining 5s, 7s, 2s, 4s and 8s be placed?*

(The answers are given below.)

Answers

In rows *A, B, C,*

the remaining 7 must be in cell *Ch*

the remaining 1 must be in cell *Bd*

the remaining 8s must be in cells *Ai* and *Ba*

the remaining 2s must be in cells *Ag* and *Cc*

In rows *G, H, I,*

the remaining 5 must be in cell *Ga*

the remaining 7 must be in cell *He*

the remaining 2 must be in cell *Ie*

the remaining 4s must be in cells *Ia* and *Hi*

the remaining 8s must be in cells *If* and *Gb*

10. Scanning the columns

Our grid is now as follows:

	a	b	c	d	e	f	g	h	i
A	9	5		4		7	2	1	8
B	8	7	4	1		2	9	6	5
C		1	2	8	9	5	4	7	
D	2				8		5	9	1
E	1			2	5	3			6
F		4	5		1				2
G	5	8	7		4	1		2	
H	3	2		9	7		8	5	4
I	4	6		5	2	8			7

We can also carry out a similar process for the columns.

In columns *a*, *b*, *c* (boxes ■1■, ■4■, ■7■):

■ there are three 2s, 4s and 5s;

■ the remaining 7 cannot be in columns *b* or *c*, so must be in column *a*, in cell *Fa*;

■ the remaining 6s must be in cells *Dc* and *Ca*.

Continuing in this way we can fill in all the remaining entries in columns *a*, *b* and *c*.

We can then look at columns *d*, *e* and *f*. For example:

■ there are three 1s, 2s, 5s and 8s;

■ 4 must be in cell *Df* and 9 must be in cell *Ff*.

Finally, we can look at columns *g*, *h*, *i*. *By filling in these cells, and the remaining ones, complete our first sudoku puzzle and then check your solution with the completed grid overleaf.*

11. The completed grid

The puzzle is now complete:

	a	b	c	d	e	f	g	h	i
A	9	5	3	4	6	7	2	1	8
B	8	7	4	1	3	2	9	6	5
C	6	1	2	8	9	5	4	7	3
D	2	3	6	7	8	4	5	9	1
E	1	9	8	2	5	3	7	4	6
F	7	4	5	6	1	9	3	8	2
G	5	8	7	3	4	1	6	2	9
H	3	2	1	9	7	6	8	5	4
I	4	6	9	5	2	8	1	3	7

Check that each of the numbers from 1 to 9 appears just once in each row, once in each column, and once in each 3 x 3 box.

12. Looking back

We've just completed our first sudoku puzzle, and it's a good idea to think back on how we did it.

We first scanned the rows for numbers appearing in pairs (such as two 3s), and tried to fill in the third one.

We then carried out a similar process for the columns.

In this case, we were able to complete the puzzle, but usually we are not so fortunate. In such situations we can often make progress by looking at rows, columns or boxes that are almost complete to see whether we have enough information to complete them.

13. Filling in the gaps: 1

To illustrate the idea of 'filling in the gaps', let's
return to the grid on page 22. Here it is again.

	a	b	c	d	e	f	g	h	i
A	9	5		4		7	2	1	8
B	8	7	4	1		2	9	6	5
C		1	2	8	9	5	4	7	
D	2				8		5	9	1
E	1			2	5	3			6
F		4	5		1				2
G	5	8	7		4	1		2	
H	3	2		9	7		8	5	4
I	4	6		5	2	8			7

We can fill in a number of gaps in the puzzle
(fill in the numbers as you go down the list):

- the only number missing from row *B* is 3, so
  put 3 in cell *Be;*
- the only number now missing from column *e*
  (or box **2**) is 6, so put 6 in cell *Ae;*
- the only number now missing from row *A*
  is 3, so put 3 in cell *Ac;*
- the only number now missing from box **1**
  is 6, so put 6 in cell *Ca;*
- the only number now missing from row *C*
  (or box **3**) is 3, so put 3 in cell *Ci;*
- the only number now missing from column *a*
  is 7, so put 7 in cell *Fa;*
- the only number now missing from column *i*
  is 9, so put 9 in cell *Gi.*

14. Filling in the gaps: 2

Our grid now looks like this.

	a	b	c	d	e	f	g	h	i
A	9	5	3	4	6	7	2	1	8
B	8	7	4	1	3	2	9	6	5
C	6	1	2	8	9	5	4	7	3
D	2				8		5	9	1
E	1			2	5	3			6
F	7	4	5		1				2
G	5	8	7		4	1		2	9
H	3	2		9	7		8	5	4
I	4	6		5	2	8			7

We can now fill in some more gaps:

- the only numbers missing from column *b* are
  3 and 9 – put 3 in cell *Db* and 9 in cell *Eb;*

- the only numbers missing from row *H* are 1
  and 6 – put 6 in cell *Hf* and 1 in cell *Hc* ;

- the only numbers now missing from column *c*
  are 6, 8 and 9 – put 6 in cell *Dc*, 9 in cell *c*
  and 8 in cell *Ec;*

- the only numbers now missing from row *D* are
  4 and 7 – put 7 in cell *Dd* and 4 in cell *Df;*

- the only number now missing from column *f*
  is 9 – put 9 in cell *Ff.*

By filling in these cells, and the remaining gaps,
complete the puzzle and then check your
solution with the completed grid on page 24.

15. Three-in-a-line

Before we apply these ideas to a second puzzle, we need to adapt our scanning procedure to deal with a particular situation that arises from time to time. We shall need it later.

When a puzzle contains a box with three filled-in cells in a row or column we can modify our scanning procedure as follows.

Take a look at the following three rows of a puzzle, in which box **3** has 5-6-7 in one row.

	a	b	c	d	e	f	g	h	i
A								9	
B				1		3	5	6	7
C		4							

Look at the number 4. In box **1**, it appears in row C. Where else does it appear?

- In box **3**, 4 cannot be in row *B*, so must be in
  row *A* (in cell *Ag* or *Ai* – we don't know which).
- So in box **2**, 4 must be in row *B*, in cell *Be*.

A similar approach works in some situations where
we have an 'implied three-in-a-line'. To understand
what this means look at this arrangement of rows.

Look at the number 8. In box **7**, it appears in
row *G*. Where else can it appear?
- In box **8**, 8 cannot be in row *H* (because of
  the 8 in cell *Fe*), so must be in row *I*.
- So in box **9**, 8 must be in row *H*, in cell *Hi*.

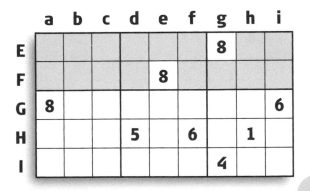

16. A new puzzle: 1

Let's work through another puzzle in full, but at each stage we'll choose whichever method seems most appropriate at the time. The grid is as follows:

	a	b	c	d	e	f	g	h	i
A	8		6			3	9		1
B		7			1	6		8	
C			9	4			2		
D		8	3		5				4
E		4		2		7		9	
F	6				9		5	1	
G			2			8	6		
H		6		5	7			3	
I	1		5	3			4		8

Since you're now more familiar with the ideas, we'll give less explanation in what follows. Begin by scanning the rows for pairs.

In rows *A*, *B*, *C*, we can put
■ 9 in cell *Bd*, 8 in cell *Ce* and 1 in cell *Cb*.

In rows *D*, *E*, *F*, we can put
■ 9 in cell *Da*, 4 in cell *Ff* and 5 in cell *Ea*.

In rows *G*, *H*, *I*, we can put
■ 8 in cell *Hc* and 6 in cell *Ie*.

Fill in all these cells.

(Incidentally, there are also several instances of three-in-a-line – for example, in rows *A*, *B*, *C*, we could put 2 in cells *Ae* and *Ba*.)

17. A new puzzle: 2

Our grid should now look like this.

	a	b	c	d	e	f	g	h	i
A	8		6			3	9		1
B		7		9	1	6		8	
C		1	9	4	8		2		
D	9	8	3		5				4
E	5	4		2		7		9	
F	6				9	4	5	1	
G			2			8	6		
H		6	8	5	7			3	
I	1		5	3	6		4		8

Now scan the columns for pairs.

In columns *a*, *b*, *c*, we already have three 6s and three 8s, and we can put
■ 5 in cell *Ab* and 1 in cell *Ec*.

In columns *d*, *e*, *f*, we can put
■ 3 in cell *Ee*, 5 in cell *Cf*, 7 in cell *Ad* and 8 in cell *Fd*.

In columns *g*, *h*, *i*, we can put
■ 1 in cell *Hg*, 8 in cell *Eg* and 4 in cell *Ah*.

Fill in all these cells as you go down the list.

(Again, there are also some instances of three-in-a-line, and some other entries we could make.)

18. A new puzzle: 3

Our grid now looks like this.

	a	b	c	d	e	f	g	h	i
A	8	5	6	7		3	9	4	1
B		7		9	1	6		8	
C		1	9	4	8	5	2		
D	9	8	3		5				4
E	5	4	1	2	3	7	8	9	
F	6			8	9	4	5	1	
G			2			8	6		
H		6	8	5	7		1	3	
I	1		5	3	6		4		8

We now fill in the remaining gaps. This can be
done in many ways – indeed, you may already
have filled in some of these cells:

- complete row *A* and box **2** with 2 in cell *Ae;*
- complete row *E* with 6 in cell *Ei;*
- complete column *e* with 4 in cell *Ge;*
- complete box **4** with 2 in cell *Fb* and 7 in
  cell *Fc;*
- complete column *c* with 4 in cell *Bc;*
- complete box **1** with 2 in cell *Ba*, and 3 in
  cell *Ca;*
- complete row *F* with 3 in cell *Fi;*
- complete row *B* with 3 in cell *Bg* and 5 in
  cell *Bi;*
- complete column *g* with 7 in cell *Dg;*
- complete box **6** with 2 in cell *Dh.*

19. A new puzzle: 4

Here's what the grid looks like now.

	a	b	c	d	e	f	g	h	i
A	8	5	6	7	2	3	9	4	1
B	2	7	4	9	1	6	3	8	5
C	3	1	9	4	8	5	2		
D	9	8	3		5		7	2	4
E	5	4	1	2	3	7	8	9	6
F	6	2	7	8	9	4	5	1	3
G			2		4	8	6		
H		6	8	5	7		1	3	
I	1		5	3	6		4		8

Which numbers go in the remaining cells?
(The answers are given opposite, and the
completed grid is over the page)

Answers

- complete row *C* and box **3** with 6 in cell *Ch* and 7 in cell *Ci*;
- complete row *D* and box **5** with 1 in cell *Df* and 6 in cell *Dd*;
- complete column *d* with 1 in cell *Gd*;
- complete column *a* with 7 in cell *Ga* and 4 in cell *Ha*;
- complete column *h* with 5 in cell *Gh* and 7 in cell *Ih*;
- complete column *i* and box **9** with 9 in cell *Gi and 2 in cell Hi*;
- complete row *G* with 3 in cell *Gb*;
- complete row *H* with 9 in cell *Hf*;
- complete row *I*, columns *b* and *f*, and boxes **7** and **8** with 9 in cell *Ib* and 2 in cell *If*.

This completes the grid.

20. The completed grid

So here is our completed grid.

	a	b	c	d	e	f	g	h	i
A	8	5	6	7	2	3	9	4	1
B	2	7	4	9	1	6	3	8	5
C	3	1	9	4	8	5	2	6	7
D	9	8	3	6	5	1	7	2	4
E	5	4	1	2	3	7	8	9	6
F	6	2	7	8	9	4	5	1	3
G	7	3	2	1	4	8	6	5	9
H	4	6	8	5	7	9	1	3	2
I	1	9	5	3	6	2	4	7	8

21. Time to take a breather

We've just completed another sudoku puzzle.
You might want to take a break and look back
over the solution of the previous puzzle to check
that you understand the ideas involved.

If you want to be absolutely sure that you've got
it, go through it again on your own. Then, when
you're ready, have a go at the puzzles on the
next four pages.

22. Practice puzzles A–D

Puzzle A

1	2		3	4			5	
		6	1					3
	7				5		1	8
		1		7		8		
4	3		6		8		9	1
		2		3		5		
8	1		4				2	
6					2	9		
	9			5	3		6	7

Puzzle B

1	2	3	4					5
			1			4	8	
		9	5			3		6
7		6		8	2		9	
3								4
	1		7	9		6		8
2		4			3	1		
	6	5			1			
8					6	2	5	7

Puzzle C

		2			6	1	4	
7	3			2	5		8	
8			9					5
2	9			4		8		
	1		5		8		7	
		8		1			6	9
5					3			2
	2		8	5			1	7
	4	6	2			3		

Puzzle D

	3	1				5	8	
		9	4		1	7		
			9		8			
8	7		3		5		9	2
1	5		6		9		4	7
			5		3			
		4	1		7	8		
	6	5				2	1	

23. Solutions to puzzles A–D

Puzzle A

1	2	8	3	4	7	6	5	9
5	4	6	1	8	9	2	7	3
3	7	9	2	6	5	4	1	8
9	6	1	5	7	4	8	3	2
4	3	5	6	2	8	7	9	1
7	8	2	9	3	1	5	4	6
8	1	7	4	9	6	3	2	5
6	5	3	7	1	2	9	8	4
2	9	4	8	5	3	1	6	7

Puzzle B

1	2	3	4	6	8	9	7	5
6	5	7	1	3	9	4	8	2
4	8	9	5	2	7	3	1	6
7	4	6	3	8	2	5	9	1
3	9	8	6	1	5	7	2	4
5	1	2	7	9	4	6	3	8
2	7	4	8	5	3	1	6	9
9	6	5	2	7	1	8	4	3
8	3	1	9	4	6	2	5	7

Puzzle C

9	5	2	7	8	6	1	4	3
7	3	1	4	2	5	9	8	6
8	6	4	9	3	1	7	2	5
2	9	5	6	4	7	8	3	1
6	1	3	5	9	8	2	7	4
4	7	8	3	1	2	5	6	9
5	8	7	1	6	3	4	9	2
3	2	9	8	5	4	6	1	7
1	4	6	2	7	9	3	5	8

Puzzle D

4	3	1	2	7	6	5	8	9
5	8	9	4	3	1	7	2	6
6	2	7	9	5	8	4	3	1
8	7	6	3	4	5	1	9	2
9	4	3	7	1	2	6	5	8
1	5	2	6	8	9	3	4	7
2	1	8	5	6	3	9	7	4
3	9	4	1	2	7	8	6	5
7	6	5	8	9	4	2	1	3

Part 3

Further tips

24. Some general principles

Up to this point we've systematically scanned the rows and columns in order, and then filled the gaps in the rows, columns and boxes.

This can work well when the puzzle has many completed cells to start with, but take a look at the puzzle opposite (which we'll solve later). You'll notice that we can't make much progress using our previous methods!

So in this part we'll shift our attention from the rows, columns and boxes to the individual cells, and investigate which numbers can fill those cells.

			3		6		
4		5	8			1		
6		7	9					8
		4						
			1	2	3			
						7		
7					1	5		2
		6			7	8		9
		8		4				

To illustrate the ideas we'll return to our first
puzzle (which we solved on pages 16–24) and
solve it in a completely different way. By
combining the two approaches you'll be able to
solve a much wider range of sudoku puzzles than
you've been able to so far.

25. Filling in single cells: 1

Here's our first puzzle again:

	a	b	c	d	e	f	g	h	i
A	9					7		1	
B		7	4			2		6	5
C		1		8	9		4		
D	2				8		5	9	
E	1			2		3			6
F		4	5		1				2
G			7		4	1		2	
H	3	2		9			8	5	
I		6		5					7

Which numbers can be placed in cell Hc?

■ not 3, 2, 9, 8 or 5, which are in the same row;
■ not 4, 5 or 7, which are in the same column;
■ not 3, 2, 6 or 7, which are in the same box.

The only remaining possibility is 1.

In the same way, we can work out which numbers can be placed in some other cells.

Questions

Which number must be placed:

(i)   *in cell Be?*

(ii) *in cell Ci?*

(iii) *in cell Hf?*

(iv) *in cell Db?*

Answers

(i) 3 (ii) 3 (iii) 6 (iv) 3

26. Filling in single cells: 2

Once we've filled in these cells our grid looks like this.

	a	b	c	d	e	f	g	h	i
A	9					7		1	
B		7	4		3	2		6	5
C		1		8	9		4		3
D	2	3			8		5	9	
E	1			2		3			6
F		4	5		1				2
G			7		4	1		2	
H	3	2	1	9		6	8	5	
I		6		5					7

We can now fill in some more cells.

Question

Which number must be placed

(i)   *in cell Cf?*

(ii) *in cell Bg?*

To locate those cells that can be filled in like this we need to look for cells with eight different numbers appearing in the same row, column and box (if there are any). This will soon become automatic with practice.

Question

(iii) *Which other single cells can be filled in?*

Answers

(i) 5; (ii) 9;

(iii) *Ag* (2), *Ai* (8), *Ba* (8), *Bd* (1), *Ch* (7), *Df* (4), *Eg* (7), *Ff* (9), *Gi* (9), *He* (7), *Hi* (4), *Ie* (2), *If* (8).

27. Filling in single cells: 3

The grid looks like this after filling in these cells.

	a	b	c	d	e	f	g	h	i
A	9					7	2	1	8
B	8	7	4	1	3	2	9	6	5
C		1		8	9	5	4	7	3
D	2	3			8	4	5	9	
E	1			2		3	7		6
F		4	5		1	9			2
G			7		4	1		2	9
H	3	2	1	9	7	6	8	5	4
I		6		5	2	8			7

We can now fill in several more cells.

Question

Which cells can now be filled in?

(The answer is given below.)

When you've answered this, fill them in and complete the puzzle.

The solution's given on the next page.

Answer

Ab (5), *Ad* (4), *Ae* (6), *Ca* (6), *Di* (1), *Ee* (5), *Fg* (3), *Gd* (3), *Ic* (9), *Ih* (3).

28. The completed grid

Here's what the solution looks like.

	a	b	c	d	e	f	g	h	i
A	9	5	3	4	6	7	2	1	8
B	8	7	4	1	3	2	9	6	5
C	6	1	2	8	9	5	4	7	3
D	2	3	6	7	8	4	5	9	1
E	1	9	8	2	5	3	7	4	6
F	7	4	5	6	1	9	3	8	2
G	5	8	7	3	4	1	6	2	9
H	3	2	1	9	7	6	8	5	4
I	4	6	9	5	2	8	1	3	7

29. Zooming in on the action

So far we've been fairly systematic in our approach, scanning the rows and columns in order, and then working through the boxes. In practice, for many puzzles it's not necessary to be so systematic.

You'll soon become adept at looking at a problem and 'zooming in on the action'. This means focusing on those parts of the puzzle where you're most likely to make progress – rows or columns with many pairs, or rows, columns and boxes with the largest number of completed cells.

In general, you're more likely to make progress in those parts of a puzzle where the numbers are dense than where they're sparse.

30. A harder puzzle: 1

We'll now look at a harder puzzle that can be
solved by combining our previous methods with
our new technique of 'filling in single cells'.
Here's the next grid.

	a	b	c	d	e	f	g	h	i
A					3		6		
B	4		5	8			1		
C	6		7	9					8
D			4						
E				1	2	3			
F							7		
G	7					1	5		2
H			6			7	8		9
I			8		4				

There are many ways of solving this puzzle.
Here's just one way of approaching the problem.

As usual, we start by scanning the rows and
columns:
- in row *G*, put 8 in cell *Ge*;
- in column *e*, put 1 in cell *Ce*.

There's a three-in-a-line in row *E*:
- in rows *D, E, F*, 7 must be in cell *Dd* or *De*, so
  we can put 7 in cell *Eb*.

We now look for single cells that we can fill in:
- cell *Ec* cannot contain 1, 2, 3, 4, 5, 6, 7 or 8,
  so put 9 in cell *Ec*;
- cell *Eg* cannot now contain 1, 2, 3, 5, 6, 7, 8
  or 9, so put 4 in cell *Eg*.

31. A harder puzzle: 2

Our grid now looks like this.

	a	b	c	d	e	f	g	h	i
A					3		6		
B	4		5	8			1		
C	6		7	9	1				8
D			4						
E		7	9	1	2	3	4		
F							7		
G	7				8	1	5		2
H			6			7	8		9
I			8		4				

We can now fill in some more cells.

- In column *g*, 2, 3 and 9 are missing:
  only 3 can be put in cell *Ig*, then 2 in cell *Cg*
  and 9 in cell *Dg*.
- The only possibility for cell *Gc* is 3, and for
  cell *He* is 5.
- In row *H* put 3 in cell *Hd*.
- 2, 6 and 9 are missing from box **8**:
  only 6 can be put in cell *Gd*.
- Complete row *G* with 4 in cell *Gh* and 9 in
  cell *Gb*.
- In column *a*, put 9 in cell *Aa*, and then in row
  B put 9 in cell *Bh*.
- 1, 2, 3 and 8 are missing from box **1**:
  only 3 can be put in cell *Cb*, then 2 in cell *Bb*,
  then 1 in cell *Ac* and 8 in cell *Ab*.
- Complete column *c* with 2 in cell *Fc*.

32. A harder puzzle: 3

Our grid looks like this now.

	a	b	c	d	e	f	g	h	i
A	9	8	1		3		6		
B	4	2	5	8			1	9	
C	6	3	7	9	1		2		8
D			4				9		
E		7	9	1	2	3	4		
F			2				7		
G	7	9	3	6	8	1	5	4	2
H			6	3	5	7	8		9
I			8		4		3		

We'll carry on like this, but from now on the
explanations will be more concise since you
should be in the groove by now.

Further cells can be filled in as follows:

■ complete row *C* with 5 in cell *Ch* and 4 in cell *Cf*;

■ complete box **3** with 3 in cell *Bi*, 7 in cell *Ah*
and 4 in cell *Ai*;

■ complete box **9** with 1 in cell *Hh*, 6 in cell *Ih*
and 7 in cell *Ii*;

■ complete row *H* with 2 in cell *Ha* and 4 in cell *Hb*;

■ complete box **8** with 2 in cell *Id* and 9 in
cell *If*;

■ complete row *A* with 5 in cell *Ad* and 2 in cell *Af*;

■ complete row *B* and box **2** with 6 in cell *Bf*
and 7 in cell *Be*;

■ complete column *d* with 7 in cell *Dd* and 4 in
cell *Fd*.

33. A harder puzzle: 4

Our grid now looks like this.

	a	b	c	d	e	f	g	h	i
A	9	8	1	5	3	2	6	7	4
B	4	2	5	8	7	6	1	9	3
C	6	3	7	9	1	4	2	5	8
D			4	7			9		
E		7	9	1	2	3	4		
F			2	4			7		
G	7	9	3	6	8	1	5	4	2
H	2	4	6	3	5	7	8	1	9
I			8	2	4	9	3	6	7

We fill in the remaining cells as follows:

- complete column *e* with 6 in cell *De* and 9 in cell *Fe*;
- complete column *h* with 8 in cell *Eh*, 3 in cell *Fh* and 2 in cell *Dh*;
- complete row *E* with 5 in cell *Ea* and 6 in cell *Ei*;
- complete row *I* and box **7** with 1 in cell *Ia* and 5 in cell *Ib*;
- complete column *a* with 8 in cell *Fa* and 3 in cell *Da*;
- complete column *b* and box **4** with 1 in cell *Db* and 6 in cell *Fb*;
- complete column *f* and box **5** with 5 in cell *Ff* and 8 in cell *Df*;
- finally, complete rows *D* and *F*, column *i* and box **6** with 5 in cell *Di* and 1 in cell *Fi*.

34. The completed grid

Take a look at the finished puzzle.

	a	b	c	d	e	f	g	h	i
A	9	8	1	5	3	2	6	7	4
B	4	2	5	8	7	6	1	9	3
C	6	3	7	9	1	4	2	5	8
D	3	1	4	7	6	8	9	2	5
E	5	7	9	1	2	3	4	8	6
F	8	6	2	4	9	5	7	3	1
G	7	9	3	6	8	1	5	4	2
H	2	4	6	3	5	7	8	1	9
I	1	5	8	2	4	9	3	6	7

35. Time to recover

That was quite a marathon – yet the steps we took at each stage are ones that should already be familiar to you. As you'll have seen, the main difficulty is in searching the grid to decide which step to take next.

At this stage you might like to go back and see whether you can solve this puzzle again on your own – then check your solution against the one here. It's very likely that your mode of attack is different from ours, and it may even be quicker.

When you've done that, try the following problems. All can be completed in a similar way to the puzzle we've just solved.

36. Practice puzzles E–H

Puzzle E

5						4		
	8			3			9	6
3					9		8	7
	4	9	1					
6				2				5
					3	9	6	
9	6		3					1
8	1			6			7	
		4						3

Puzzle F

5			1		3			8
	1			5			4	
	2						9	
	3	8	7		2	9	5	
	4						2	
	5	7	9		8	6	3	
	6						8	
	7			9			1	
4			6		5			9

Puzzle G

3			8		2			1
1		2		3		6		4
			1		4			
8		9				2		6
	6						5	
7		1				4		9
			5		9			
9		4		8		7		5
6			2		7			3

Puzzle H

		7			1	9	4	
3	2		6	5			7	
9								5
4							9	
	3			9			2	
	8							4
6								2
	9			7	6		8	1
	1	8	4			3		

37. Solutions to puzzles E-H

Puzzle E

5	9	7	6	1	8	4	3	2
4	8	1	2	3	7	5	9	6
3	2	6	5	4	9	1	8	7
7	4	9	1	5	6	3	2	8
6	3	8	9	2	4	7	1	5
1	5	2	7	8	3	9	6	4
9	6	5	3	7	2	8	4	1
8	1	3	4	6	5	2	7	9
2	7	4	8	9	1	6	5	3

Puzzle F

5	9	4	1	7	3	2	6	8
8	1	6	2	5	9	7	4	3
7	2	3	4	8	6	1	9	5
1	3	8	7	6	2	9	5	4
6	4	9	5	3	1	8	2	7
2	5	7	9	4	8	6	3	1
9	6	5	3	1	7	4	8	2
3	7	2	8	9	4	5	1	6
4	8	1	6	2	5	3	7	9

Puzzle G

3	4	6	8	9	2	5	7	1
1	9	2	7	3	5	6	8	4
5	7	8	1	6	4	3	9	2
8	5	9	4	7	3	2	1	6
4	6	3	9	2	1	8	5	7
7	2	1	6	5	8	4	3	9
2	3	7	5	4	9	1	6	8
9	1	4	3	8	6	7	2	5
6	8	5	2	1	7	9	4	3

Puzzle H

8	5	7	2	3	1	9	4	6
3	2	4	6	5	9	1	7	8
9	6	1	8	4	7	2	3	5
4	7	5	1	8	2	6	9	3
1	3	6	5	9	4	8	2	7
2	8	9	7	6	3	5	1	4
6	4	3	9	1	8	7	5	2
5	9	2	3	7	6	4	8	1
7	1	8	4	2	5	3	6	9

38. Solving even harder puzzles

As you've seen, so long as we use enough ingenuity we can solve a wide range of sudoku puzzles. However, there are even harder problems that do not yield to the range of techniques we've used so far. In these cases we are reduced to more desperate measures.

A standard method is to record the possibilities for each cell by writing smaller numbers in the cells. For example, if we know that a given cell must contain 2, 4 or 5, we can write these numbers at the top of the cell. Later in the process we may be able to eliminate the number 4, so we cross it out. If we can subsequently eliminate 2 as well, then we are left with 5, which can then be written in the cell.

Some people carry this further by writing every possible number in each cell and then systematically crossing out all those that can be eliminated. This needs a magnified grid and can also take a lot of time. With practice, you'll learn to combine this idea with earlier methods in an efficient and effective way.

An alternative idea is to insert these smaller numbers whenever you locate a pair of cells that (between them) must contain a given number. For example, if you know that 7 must appear in cell *Aa* or *Ab*, you can write 7 at the top of these two cells. Unfortunately, there seems to be no convenient way of keeping track of all these pairs, so we won't use this method here.

Shortly you will see how we can use the smaller numbers technique to solve a difficult sudoku puzzle. But first, here's a useful observation on a feature of sudoku solving we call 'twins and triplets'.

39. Twins and triplets

One advantage of using these little numbers is that they will help us to look for *twins* and *triplets*. This gives us a very effective method of reducing the possibilities.

To see what we mean by this, look at the following three rows in which the possible entries for several cells have been written in.

	a	b	c	d	e	f	g	h	i
A		35	35		37			359	
B	46	678		468		68			69
C									

In row *A*, look at cells *Ab* and *Ac*. Between them they must 'use up' the numbers 3 and 5 in row *A*. It follows that neither 3 nor 5 can appear anywhere else in this row (in particular, in cell *Ae* or *Ah*), and thus any 3s or 5s can be crossed out from these cells (such numbers are called *twins*).

By the way, the same thing applies to twins that appear in the same column, or in the same box.

We can go further. In row *B*, look at cells *Ba*, *Bd* and *Bf* – between them they must 'use up' the numbers 4, 6 and 8 in row *B*. It follows that none of 4, 6 and 8 can appear anywhere else in this row (in particular, in cell *Bb* or *Bi*), and thus any 4s, 6s or 8s can be crossed out from these cells (such numbers are called *triplets*).

You'll soon become used to spotting twins and triplets and using them effectively.

40. Our final puzzle: 1

In our final puzzle we shall use these smaller numerals. Here's the grid.

	a	b	c	d	e	f	g	h	i
A			4				6		
B		2		4		3		1	
C	1			8		9			4
D		7			5			6	
E				2	3	8			
F		1			9			5	
G	5			3		6			7
H		9		7		5		2	
I			7				8		

As usual, first scan the rows and columns:

■ in row *I*, put 5 in cell *Ii*;

■ in column *d*, put 5 in cell *Ad* and 9 in cell *Id*;

■ in column *i*, put 6 in cell *Hi*.

Now complete column *d*:

■ in column *d*, put 6 in cell *Fd* and 1 in cell *Dd*.

We can also complete box **5**:

■ in row *D*, put 7 in cell *Ff* and 4 in cell *Df*.

We could also have found the 7 in cell *Ff* and then the 6 in cell *Fd* by using the fact that row *E* has a three-in-a-line.

■ in columns *g*, *h* and *i*, there is an implied three-in-a-line: we cannot put 8 in cell *Eh*, so the 8 in box **6** must be in column i, in cell *Di* or *Fi*, and the 8 in box **3** must be in column *h*, in cell *Ah*.

41. Our final puzzle: 2

Now the grid looks like this.

	a	b	c	d	e	f	g	h	i
A			4	5			6	8	
B		2		4		3		1	
C	1			8		9			4
D		7		1	5	4		6	
E				2	3	8			
F		1		6	9	7		5	
G	5			3		6			7
H		9		7		5		2	6
I			7	9			8		5

Before we insert the little numbers, there are a few more cells that we can fill in:

■ in column *b*, the only cell into which we can put 8 is cell *Gb*;

■ we can now put 8 in cell *He*;

■ the only possibility for cell *Bi* is 9, and we can also put 9 in cell *Aa*;

■ the only possibility for cell *Ab* is 3.

We could carry on further in this way, but instead let's measure our progress by writing little numbers at the top of each cell to indicate the possible numbers for that cell. (This could have been done at any earlier stage, or for just a few selected cells.) The result is given on the next page.

42. Our final puzzle: 3

Our grid now looks like this.

	a	b	c	d	e	f	g	h	i
A	9	3	4	5	127	12	6	8	2
B	678	2	568	4	67	3	57	1	9
C	1	56	56	8	267	9	2357	37	4
D	238	7	2389	1	5	4	239	6	238
E	46	456	569	2	3	8	1479	479	1
F	2348	1	238	6	9	7	234	5	238
G	5	8	12	3	124	6	149	49	7
H	34	9	13	7	8	5	134	2	6
I	2346	46	7	9	124	12	8	349	5

These little numbers indicate several places where we can immediately make progress:

- we must put 2 in cell *Ai* and 1 in cell *Ei*;
- after crossing out the little 2 in cells *Ae* and *Af*, we must put 1 in cell *Af*, then 2 in cell *If* and 7 in cell *Ae*;
- we can then put 6 in cell *Be* and 2 in cell *Ce*;
- when we cross out the little 2s in cells *Di* and *Fi*, these two cells become twins containing 3 and 8 (in some order), which we then cross out from the other cells in box **6**;
- the cells *Cb* and *Cc* are twins containing 5 and 6, so cell *Bc* contains 8 and cell *Ba* contains 7 – we can then put 5 in cell *Bg*.

At each stage we cross out any of the little numbers that no longer apply.

43. Our final puzzle: 4

Nearly complete, it looks like this.

	a	b	c	d	e	f	g	h	i
A	9	3	4	5	7	1	6	8	2
B	7	2	8	4	6	3	5	1	9
C	1	56	56	8	2	9	37	37	4
D	238	7	239	1	5	4	29	6	38
E	46	456	569	2	3	8	479	479	1
F	2348	1	23	6	9	7	24	5	38
G	5	8	12	3	14	6	149	49	7
H	34	9	13	7	8	5	134	2	6
I	346	46	7	9	14	2	8	34	5

We can continue as follows:

- cells *Fc*, *Gc* and *Hc* form a triplet that use up 1, 2, 3 – so (after crossing out 1, 2, 3 from column *c*) we can put 9 in cell *Dc* and 2 in cell *Dg*;
- the only possibility for cell *Fg* is now 4;
- in row *G*, the only cell in which 2 can appear is cell *Gc* – so we can put 3 in cell *Fc* and 1 in cell *Hc*;
- we can now put 8 in cell *Fi* and 3 in cell *Di*.

Carrying on in this way we can now easily complete the puzzle – the solution is shown on the next page.

44. The completed grid

The finished puzzle looks like this.

	a	b	c	d	e	f	g	h	i
A	9	3	4	5	7	1	6	8	2
B	7	2	8	4	6	3	5	1	9
C	1	5	6	8	2	9	7	3	4
D	8	7	9	1	5	4	2	6	3
E	6	4	5	2	3	8	9	7	1
F	2	1	3	6	9	7	4	5	8
G	5	8	2	3	4	6	1	9	7
H	4	9	1	7	8	5	3	2	6
I	3	6	7	9	1	2	8	4	5

45. Recovering

Using these little numbers you should now be able to solve all but the most difficult sudoku puzzles.

At this stage you might like to go back and see whether you can solve this puzzle again on your own, and then check your solution with the one we gave. As before, it's very likely that the way you handle it will differ from the route taken here, and it may be quicker.

When you've done that, try the following problems. None of them is easy, but they can all be completed in a similar way.

46. Practice puzzles I–L

Puzzle I

	1				3			
	3			8			4	6
		7				2		
6			8		1			
	8			3			5	
			4		7			9
		6				5		
5	7			2			9	
			1				7	

Puzzle J

		6	5					
	1	8					7	
	9		3					2
2							4	7
			6		1			
8	3							6
1					6		8	
	5					1	3	
					2	7		

Puzzle K

	1	2	3					
8					4	5	6	
9							7	
7			5				8	
	4				2			9
	3							1
	5	7	9					4
					6	8	2	

Puzzle L

	6			7			2	
		5				4		
1				6				7
		4	8		5	2		
				1				
		8	6		9	3		
2				9				5
		6				1		
	8			4			3	

47. Solutions to puzzles I–L

Puzzle I

4	1	2	5	6	3	9	8	7
9	3	5	7	8	2	1	4	6
8	6	7	9	1	4	2	3	5
6	5	4	8	9	1	7	2	3
7	8	9	2	3	6	4	5	1
1	2	3	4	5	7	8	6	9
2	4	6	3	7	9	5	1	8
5	7	1	6	2	8	3	9	4
3	9	8	1	4	5	6	7	2

Puzzle J

3	2	6	5	4	7	8	9	1
5	1	8	2	6	9	4	7	3
7	9	4	3	1	8	6	5	2
2	6	1	8	9	3	5	4	7
9	4	5	6	7	1	3	2	8
8	3	7	4	2	5	9	1	6
1	7	3	9	5	6	2	8	4
6	5	2	7	8	4	1	3	9
4	8	9	1	3	2	7	6	5

Puzzle K

5	1	2	3	6	7	9	4	8
8	7	3	1	9	4	5	6	2
9	6	4	2	5	8	1	7	3
7	2	9	5	1	3	4	8	6
3	8	5	6	4	9	2	1	7
1	4	6	8	7	2	3	5	9
6	3	8	4	2	5	7	9	1
2	5	7	9	8	1	6	3	4
4	9	1	7	3	6	8	2	5

Puzzle L

8	6	9	4	7	1	5	2	3
3	7	5	9	8	2	4	6	1
1	4	2	5	6	3	8	9	7
9	1	4	8	3	5	2	7	6
6	2	3	7	1	4	9	5	8
7	5	8	6	2	9	3	1	4
2	3	7	1	9	8	6	4	5
4	9	6	3	5	7	1	8	2
5	8	1	2	4	6	7	3	9

48. What if I get stuck?

If you get stuck while attempting a sudoku puzzle, there are a number of things that you can try:

■ scan all the rows and columns carefully again, looking at each number from 1 to 9 in turn to see whether you can fill in another square;

■ look for a three-in-a-line, or an implied three-in-a-line;

■ look at all rows, columns and boxes that have several (say, five or more) filled-in cells and investigate those numbers that still have to be inserted;

■ concentrate particularly on numbers that occur frequently in the grid as a whole, or on those parts of the grid that have a lot of filled-in cells;

- write in the little numbers, and use them to locate those cells that have the fewest number of possible entries;
- look particularly for twins and triplets, and use them to reduce the numbers of possibilities for other cells in the same row, column or box;
- take a break and come back to the puzzle with a fresh mind;
- if you're really desperate, choose a cell with as few little numbers as possible and work through the possibilities one at a time to see the consequences of choosing each – you may be able to eliminate some of them;
- (not recommended) look up the solution at the back of the book or wait for the next day's newspaper.

Part 4
Last words

49. Latin squares

Several writers have incorrectly credited the eighteenth-century Swiss mathematician Leonhard Euler with the invention of sudoku.

Euler certainly studied *Latin squares* – *n* x *n* grids of numbers in which the numbers from 1 to *n* appear just once in each row and column. For example, here is a Latin square of size 9 x 9:

1	2	3	4	5	6	7	8	9
2	3	1	5	6	4	8	9	7
3	1	2	6	4	5	9	7	8
4	5	6	7	8	9	1	2	3
5	6	4	8	9	7	2	3	1
6	4	5	9	7	8	3	1	2
7	8	9	1	2	3	4	5	6
8	9	7	2	3	1	5	6	4
9	7	8	3	1	2	6	4	5

Thus, a Latin square is like a completed sudoku grid, but without the extra condition on the boxes: every completed sudoku grid is a Latin square, but not every Latin square corresponds to a completed sudoku grid, as the example opposite shows.

There are many more Latin squares than sudoku grids. In fact, the number of possible Latin squares of size 9 x 9 can be shown to be

5,524,751,496,156,892,842,531,225,600

whereas the number of possible sudoku patterns is believed to be a mere

6,670,903,752,021,072,936,960

Euler's work on Latin squares arose from his study of 'magic squares' (a different type of mathematical object which is beyond the scope of this book) and several writers on sudoku have confused the two.

50. Computers and sudoku

Computers arise in the sudoku story in the construction of sudoku puzzles and their solution.

As we saw in the introductory part of this book, the construction of a good sudoku puzzle is not an easy matter. The Nikoli firm in Japan prides itself on the construction of interesting and ingenious sudoku patterns by hand.

On the other hand, the problem of constructing suitable patterns is a natural thing to program on a computer, and there are many such programs around the world that churn out sudoku patterns by the score (of varying complexity and quality).

At the other end of the story is the use of computers to solve sudoku puzzles. A search of the internet will yield a large number of computer programs that claim to solve any sudoku puzzle that is presented.

The existence of such a variety of computer programs is hardly surprising. The number of possible ways of completing a given sudoku grid is large, but a computer can work through them systematically and often produce the solution in a very short time.

While designing these programs may be very interesting, their benefit to us is doubtful. It is surely much more satisfying to solve sudoku puzzles by hand (after all, that is the whole point), using the methods in this book together with others that you may have devised on your own.

51. Variations on sudoku

Once sudoku began to take hold, it was
inevitable that a wide variety of sudoku-type
puzzles should spring up.

Some variations use grids of different sizes. At one
end of the scale are puzzles with smaller grids,
such as a 4 x 4 grid divided into four 2 x 2 boxes.
These are usually very easy, so some newspapers,
eager to tempt people into the world of sudoku
without subjecting them to the full 9 x 9 grid,
have presented 'warm-up puzzles' consisting of a
6 x 6 grid made up of six 2 x 3 rectangular boxes.

At the other end of the scale are puzzles that
use larger grids. One newspaper sets a weekly
sudoku competition involving a 16 x 16 grid
divided into sixteen 4 x 4 boxes, and some
puzzles have been set with 25 x 25 grids, divided
into twenty-five 5 x 5 boxes.

	A	B	C	D	E	F	G	H	I	J		K			
F	O					J			K		C	E			M
I			L	M					G						
J							L	E			P			G	
		A	B	K				G	D	M		O	L	I	J
H	L	C					O		P	E		G	A	D	N
	M							F					H		B
	K	P			I	A		L							C
M				L		P		O	E	D			J		
	F	J		C	O	I	K	B				D			
D		K	O		N	H	E	J	M	C	G				
	E		P		G		M	K							
			N				D	M				C		A	
				P	B					F		L	G		H
			M				J			C	K		I	B	N
B	C	L	G	A				P					J		O

Here is a 16 x 16 puzzle for you to try; its solution is on page 107.

Another variation is the construction and solution of sudoku puzzles in which each of the numbers from 1 to 9 must appear in each row, column and box, as before, but also on the two diagonals of the square grid.

Finally, it is not necessary to restrict ourselves to two-dimensional puzzles. A puzzle enthusiast named Dion Church has designed a three-dimensional version – the *Dion cube* – in which each slice through the cube (in each of the three dimensions) yields a valid sudoku pattern.

You might like to try to designing some interesting variations of your own...

N	A	B	C	D	E	F	G	H	I	J	M	K	P	L	O
F	G	O	H	P	A	J	I	N	K	L	C	E	D	B	M
I	P	E	L	M	C	K	B	F	G	O	D	H	N	J	A
J	D	M	K	O	H	N	L	E	A	B	P	F	C	G	I
E	N	A	B	K	F	C	P	G	D	M	H	O	L	I	J
H	L	C	F	B	J	M	O	I	P	E	K	G	A	D	N
G	M	I	J	E	D	L	N	C	F	A	O	P	H	K	B
O	K	P	D	G	I	A	H	L	J	N	B	M	E	F	C
M	H	G	I	L	B	P	A	O	E	D	F	N	J	C	K
L	F	J	A	C	O	I	K	B	H	P	N	D	M	E	G
D	B	K	O	F	N	H	E	J	M	C	G	A	I	P	L
C	E	N	P	J	G	D	M	K	L	I	A	B	O	H	F
P	J	H	N	I	K	O	D	M	B	G	L	C	F	A	E
K	I	D	E	N	P	B	C	A	O	F	J	L	G	M	H
A	O	F	M	H	L	G	J	D	C	K	E	I	B	N	P
B	C	L	G	A	M	E	F	P	N	H	I	J	K	O	D

52. Find out more

Now that you have reached the end of this book, you may wish to hone your sudoku skills further. There are several books that provide many puzzles for you to practice on, such as *The Times Su Doku* books, compiled by Wayne Gould, and the *Daily Telegraph Sudoku* books, compiled by Michael Mepham.

There have also been several newspaper articles on sudoku puzzles and their solution – notably an article by Hugo Rifkind in *The Times* of 14 May 2005 and other articles that appeared in British newspapers around the same time. The educational uses of sudoku puzzles in school classrooms were described in *The Times Educational Supplement* of 10 June 2005.

Many websites contain information about sudoku:
http://en.wikipedia.org/wiki/Sudoku from
Wikipedia, the free encyclopedia, is particularly
informative and is updated regularly. The
websites of Wayne Gould (www.sudoku.com) and
Nikoli (www.nikoli.co.jp/en) are also worth
consulting.

Finally, it only remains to wish you all the best
with your sudoku explorations in the future.

Happy puzzling!

Brilliant communication

▪ If you enjoyed this book and find yourself cuddling it at night, please tell us. If you think this book isn't fit to use as kindling, please tell us. We value your thoughts and need your honest feedback. We know if we listen to you we'll get it right. E-mail us at listeners@infideas.com.

▪ Perhaps you have a brilliant idea of your own that our author has missed. Email us at yourauthormissedatrick@infideas.com and if it makes it in to print in a future edition or appears on our web site we'll send you four books of your choice or the cash equivalent. You'll be fully credited (if you want) so that everyone knows you've had a brilliant idea.

- Finally, if you've enjoyed one of our books why not become an Infinite Ideas Ambassador? Simply e-mail ten of your friends enlightening them about the virtues of the 52 Brilliant Ideas series and dishing out our web address: www.52brilliantideas.com. Make sure you copy us in at ambassador@infideas.com. We promise we won't contact them unless they contact us, but we'll send you a free book of your choice for every ten friends you email. Help spread the word!

We look forward to hearing from you.